D1358003

LLAMA FARMS

FUNKY FARMS

Lynn M. Stone

The Rourke Corporation, Inc.
Vero Beach, Florida 32964

PHOTO CREDITS:
© Craig Lovell: pages 7, 10, 12, 15; © Lynn M. Stone: cover, title page, pages 4, 8, 13, 17, 18, 21

EDITORIAL SERVICES:
Susan Albury

CREATIVE SERVICES:
East Coast Studios, Merritt Island, Florida

Library of Congress Cataloging-in-Publication Data

Stone, Lynn M.
    Llama farms / by Lynn M. Stone
        p. cm. — (Funky farms)
    Summary: Describes the physical characteristics and habits of llamas and how they are now raised domestically across the United States.
    ISBN 0-86593-541-6
    1. Llama farms Juvenile literature. 2. Llamas Juvenile literature. [1. Llamas.
2. Llama farms.] I. Title. II. Series: Stone, Lynn M. Funky farms.
SF401.L6S68 1999
636.2'.966—dc21   99-25303
                                                                                    CIP

Printed in the USA

CONTENTS

LLAMAS

For many years, the most likely place to see a llama (LAH muh) was in a zoo. But now you might find llamas on a neighbor's farm!

Llamas and llama farms are becoming more and more popular in the United States and Canada.

A llama looks much like a camel without a hump. A llama isn't nearly as big as its camel cousin. However, it has the camel's long neck, big, dark eyes, and two-toed feet. And, like the camel, a llama can spit chewed food at anyone who stands too close!

A male llama stands in its grassy pasture. Its hair is straighter and finer than the wool of sheep.

A llama is about four feet (1.2 meters) tall at its shoulder. It has a thick coat of hair, sometimes called wool or **fleece** (FLEESS). The hair may be brown, white, black, gray, or a mix of colors.

Llamas are closely related to **guanacos** (wah NAH koz). Guanacos are a wild member of the camel family. They live in South America. Llamas are **domesticated** (duh MESS tuh kate id), or tame.

These wild guanacos, the llama's wild ancestors, live in the high, rugged Atacam Desert in Chile.

LLAMA FARMS

Llama farmers in North America have about 130,000 llamas. They raise llamas for several reasons.

Some people raise llamas to guard their sheep. Llamas will chase away certain animals, such as coyotes, that might attack sheep.

A llama farmer holds tightly to the halter strap of an adult male llama. Adult males are kept apart from other males so that they don't fight with each other.

Other farmers raise llamas for use as pack animals. Like camels, llamas are good travelers, and they don't need to drink often.

Still other people raise llamas for pets, for their fleece, and to pull carts.

A farmer herds his llamas on the trail through Arapa Pass in the Andes Mountains of Peru. The llamas wear red woolen tassels in their ears.

Dusted by snow, a herd of alpacas passes by a mountain lake in Peru. Alpacas are smaller and have heavier coats than llamas.

Llamas, like camels, can be quite stubborn. A pack llama that is tired or trying to carry too much weight will simply lie down.

HOW LLAMA FARMS BEGAN

Perhaps 5,000 years ago, native people of Peru began to capture and tame the wild guanacos of their country.

The Peruvian farmers kept only those guanacos they liked for size, color, and behavior. Those animals had babies that were often like their parents.

In time, domesticated guanacos—our present day llamas—were usually bigger, more colorful, and calmer then wild guanacos.

Llamas pose on a pasture in the shadow of the Sisters Peaks in the Oregon Cascades. True herd animals, llamas need each other's company.

WHERE LLAMA FARMS ARE

Llama farms are now scattered around North America. The greatest number of llama farms is in the West, especially in California, Oregon, and Washington.

Some people have just a few llamas. Others have large herds.

No one should have just one llama. Llamas are very **social** (SO shul) animals. They like and need each other's company.

While guanacos wear only tan coats, llamas have coats of many colors.

RAISING LLAMAS

Llamas are kept behind fences at least four feet (1.2 meters) high. They graze on grass much of the year. In winter, farmers give llamas hay. Llamas may also get a helping of grain now and then.

Llamas are rugged animals. They can live in most kinds of weather. They rarely need more than a three-sided shelter, except in the coldest places.

At the age of about two and a half years, female llamas have their first baby. A llama can live to an age of 15 or 20 years.

Part of the enjoyment of raising llamas is visiting with them. Two youngsters make friends with a baby llama just six hours old.

19

Farmers begin training their young llamas at the age of six months. The animals are trained to accept a **halter** (HAWL tur) and be led on a rope.

Many llama farmers also raise a few **alpacas** (al PAK uhz). Alpacas are a domestic cousin of the llama. While llamas are mostly valued as pack animals, alpacas are famous for their long wool.

These balls of yarn made of llama wool will be used for sweaters and other warm clothing.

WHY LLAMAS?

The Inca people of ancient Peru needed llamas to haul their goods on mountain trails. Today, in North America, llamas are still valued as pack animals. But they are more prized for their coats and companionship. Many people raise llamas just to enter them in shows.

All llamas are the same kind of animal. Groups of llamas, however, have different lengths of hair— light, medium, and heavy. Heavy coats provide the best wool for weaving.

Llama wool, like the wool of sheep and alpacas, can be woven into sweaters or other clothes. More and more llama farmers are choosing their animals for the quality of their wool.

GLOSSARY

alpaca (al PAK uh) — a domestic relative of the llama, but smaller and with a heavier coat of wool

domesticated (duh MESS tuh kate id) — tamed rather than wild; coming from a long line of tame animals

fleece (FLEESS) — the coat of wool covering certain wool-bearing animals, such as llamas

guanaco (wah NAH ko) — a wild relative of the llama native to South America; the wild ancestor of the llama

halter (HAWL tur) — a rope or strap with a noseband, used for leading or tying an animal

social (SO shul) — liking the company and companionship of others of the same kind

INDEX

FURTHER READING

Find out more about llamas and alpacas with these helpful books and organizations:
Alpaca Owners and Breeders Association P.O. Box 1992, Estes Park, CO 80517-1992
Llama Association of North America 1800 S. Obenchain Road, Eagle Point, OR 97524
    email: llamainfo@aol.com
"Youth Lllama Project, Member's Manual," Rocky Mountain Llama and Alpaca Association
    7411 North Road 2 East Monte Vista, Colorado 81144